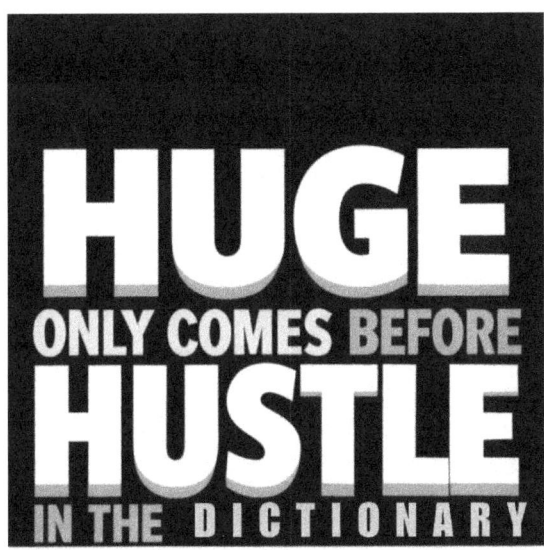

DISCLAIMER: The Author, Brian Ernest Hayward, is not a legal, financial, or medical professional, and the content provided is for informational purposes only. Always consult with a qualified professional for advice in these areas, as Brian Ernest Hayward is not responsible for any actions taken based on this information.

Copyright © 2024 by Brian Ernest Hayward and Published by Brian Hayward for Hayward House Publishing Published by Hayward House and Big Book Box A Member of the Brian Hayward Group All rights reserved. No part of this publication may be reproduced, stored in a retrieval system, or transmitted, in any form or by any means, electronic, mechanical, photocopying, recording, or otherwise, without the prior written permission of the publisher. For information and inquiries, address Hayward House publishing and Hayward Press, Savannah, Ga 31405, Library of Congress Cataloging-in-Publication Data. Hayward, Brian. TITLE=In Jesus Mighty Name Series, Journal WRITING for success in your life / Brian Hayward. p. cm.

PAPERBACK EDITION

ISBN: 9798334509719
Imprint:
Independently published

Self-control. 2. Self-management (Psychology) 3. Success. 4. Success in business. 31405, or visit us at https://www.amazon.com/Brian-Ernest-Hayward/e/B06XT464NM

PRAYER FOR MYSELF AND MY READERS

I was taught by my teacher, Pastor Bill Winston, this prayer. This prayer has served me well, and in due time it will serve you well. Father I come before you in Jesus name, thank you for the anointing that's on me and these lips of clay. I know that because of your blessing, I speak this word today with excellency, accuracy, and boldness. I thank you for thinking through my mind and speaking through my lips and this word will come forth unhindered, and unchecked by any outside force. Now I give you the praise for it and I fully expect signs, wonders, and miracles to confirm your word preached in Jesus name,

AUTHOR BIOGRAPHY

Brian Ernest Hayward is a passionate Author and Inspirational Speaker, internationally known for his unwavering dedication to creating positive change through the power of words. From religious and success books, to adult coloring books and artist BUSINESS, HOW-TO BOOKS, his writings touch on over 400 different subjects. Today, all of Brian's publications are sold worldwide across multiple formats (Paperback, Kindle, and Large Print) and are translated into 21 different languages. He has also participated in over 100 speaking engagements spanning over 38 states.

Table Of Contents

Introduction: Hustle First, Huge Later: Activate Your Natural Success Training — 6

Chapter 1: The Importance of Hustle and Discipline — 15

Chapter 2: The Essence of Hustle – Why Hard Work Comes First — 25

Chapter 3: Developing Discipline – The Backbone of Consistent Success — 33

Chapter 4: Turning on Your Natural Training – Leveraging Skills and Habits — 42

Chapter 5: Automating Discipline – Making Hard Work a Habit — 50

Chapter 6: Overcoming Obstacles – Staying Motivated and Focused — 57

Chapter 7: Measuring Progress – Tracking Your Journey to Success — 64

Chapter 8: Continuous Improvement – Enhancing Your Skills and Habits ... 71

Chapter 9: Real-Life Success Stories – Learning from the Best ... 78

Chapter 10: Sustaining Long-Term Success Through Continuous Hustle and Learning ... 85

Chapter 11: Huge Only Comes Before Hustle in the Dictionary ... 94

Chapter 12: How to Automatically Turn on Your Natural Training and Discipline to Succeed ... 101

Conclusion: Huge Success, Hustle Required: Unlock Your Natural Discipline ... 109

Bibliography ... 148

NOTES ... 149

Introduction: Hustle First, Huge Later: Activate Your Natural Success Training

Welcome to "Huge Only Comes Before Hustle in the Dictionary: How to Automatically Turn on Your Natural Training and Discipline to Succeed." This book is a comprehensive guide designed to help you harness your inherent skills and habits for remarkable success. Written over three intensive months, it is the product of dedicated research, real-life experiences, and practical insights aimed at transforming your approach to success.

In the first month, the focus was on understanding the core concepts of hustle and discipline. This involved exploring the psychology behind hard work, the importance of resilience, and

the role of consistent effort in achieving long-term goals. During this period, I delved into many success stories, analyzed the habits of high achievers, and named the common traits that contribute to sustained success.

The second month was dedicated to developing practical strategies for turning on your natural training and discipline. This involved creating actionable plans, routines, and techniques that can be easily integrated into daily life. The aim was to ensure that discipline and hard work become automatic, reducing the mental effort required to stay focused and productive. This section includes tools like time management techniques, habit stacking, and the use of technology to streamline efforts.

In the final month, the emphasis was on refining these strategies and compiling real-life examples to illustrate their effectiveness. This involved conducting interviews, gathering feedback, and making necessary adjustments to ensure the content was practical and inspiring. The goal was to create a manual that educates and motivates readers to act and apply these principles in their own lives.

The central thesis of this book is that hustle, defined as assertive, forceful, focused action to complete business goals successfully, is the foundation of all significant achievements. While the dictionary might place "huge" before "hustle," in reality, substantial success always follows hard work and dedication. This book aims to provide you with the tools and mindset needed to turn your natural training and discipline into automatic actions that drive success.

Why is this concept so crucial in today's world? In an era where distractions are rampant, and instant gratification is often prioritized, staying focused and committed to long-term goals is more important than ever. Businesses are evolving rapidly, and the need for continuous improvement and adaptability is applying. Applying the principles outlined in this book, you can develop the resilience and discipline needed to navigate these changes and achieve your goals.

The principles of "Huge Only Comes Before Hustle in the Dictionary" are indispensable in day-to-day business. Whether you're an entrepreneur building a startup, a professional climbing the corporate ladder, or a student striving for academic excellence, harnessing your natural training and discipline is critical to success. This book provides practical steps to develop and automate discipline in daily routines, ensuring that you still are focused and productive.

The first chapter, "The Importance of Hustle and Discipline," defines these concepts and illustrates their significance through compelling stories. It provides an overview of the book and introduces practical strategies for developing, automating, and applying discipline and hard work to achieve significant success.

In Chapter Two, "The Essence of Hustle—Why Hard Work Comes First," we delve deeper into the hustle concept. This chapter defines hustle in various contexts and discusses why effort is crucial in achieving significant results. It highlights real-life examples of individuals who achieved success through relentless hard work, reinforcing that hustle precedes huge accomplishments.

Chapter Three, "Developing Discipline – The Backbone of Consistent Success," explores the importance of discipline in achieving long-term goals. It provides strategies for building solid habits, managing time effectively, and supporting focus. This chapter emphasizes the role of self-control and resilience in sustaining discipline and achieving success.

In Chapter Four, "Turning on Your Natural Training—Leveraging Skills and Habits," discusses how to recognize and harness your natural skills and habits. It provides strategies for integrating these strengths into your daily routines, making discipline feel effortless. It emphasizes the importance of self-awareness and continuous improvement in using your natural training.

Chapter Five, "Automating Disciple—Making Hard Work a Habit," focuses on creating systems and routines that make hard work automatic. It provides practical techniques for building and keeping discipline and consistent and sustainable efforts. This chapter explores tools and techniques like time-blocking and habit-tracking apps to help automate and support discipline.

In Chapter Six, "Overcoming Obstacles – Staying Motivated and Focused," we address common challenges to keeping discipline and hustle. This chapter offers practical solutions for staying motivated and focused, including setting small, achievable goals and celebrating progress. It emphasizes the importance of resilience and self-care in overcoming obstacles and sustaining long-term success.

Chapter Seven, "Measuring Progress – Tracking Your Journey to Success," highlights the importance of tracking progress and adjusting strategies as needed. This chapter introduces effective methods for tracking progress, such as journaling, progress charts, and digital tools. It provides tips for analyzing progress and making necessary adjustments to stay on track.

Chapter "Continuous Improvement—Enhancing Your Skills and Habits" discusses the importance of continuously improving skills and habits to stay competitive and succeed tremendously. This chapter helps readers find areas for growth and offers strategies for incorporating continuous improvement into daily routines. It emphasizes the need for ongoing education and self-reflection.

Chapter Nine, "Real-Life Success Stories – Learning from the Best," shares inspirational stories of individuals who have exemplified hustle, discipline, and continuous improvement to achieve significant success. This chapter highlights key lessons and takeaways from these stories that readers can apply to their lives. It offers practical insights and strategies inspired by these success stories to help readers achieve their goals.

The final chapter, "Sustaining Long-Term Success Through Continuous Hustle and Learning," explores strategies for keeping long-term success through continuous hustle and learning. This chapter emphasizes the importance of consistency, adaptability, and resilience in achieving and sustaining success. It provides practical tips for staying motivated, setting new goals, and keeping a positive attitude.

In Summary, "Huge Only Comes Before Hustle in the Dictionary: How to Automatically Turn on Your Natural Training  and Discipline to Succeed" is a comprehensive guide to achieving significant success through hard work, discipline, and continuous improvement. Applying the principles outlined in this book, you can harness your natural skills and habits to achieve your goals effortlessly and sustainably. The journey to success begins with hustle, and this book provides the tools and mindset needed to make that journey a reality.

Chapter 1: The Importance of Hustle and Discipline

Success is a journey, not a destination; on this journey, hustle and discipline are your most reliable companions. Consider the story of Sam, who once struggled to balance his life and work. Sam's breakthrough came when he realized that success didn't come from sporadic bursts of hard work but from consistent  hustle and unwavering discipline. He started setting small, achievable goals and celebrated each milestone. This daily grind, paired with self-discipline, transformed his life, proving that significant success is a series of small wins compounded over time.

Hustle, in its essence, is the willingness to go the extra mile, even when it seems inconvenient. It's about waking up early, staying up late, and doing what others are unwilling to do. On the other hand, discipline is the ability to keep this hustle consistently. The internal force pushes you to keep going, even when motivation fades. Together, hustle and discipline create a powerful synergy that drives success.

The phrase "Huge Only Comes Before Hustle in the Dictionary" perfectly encapsulates this concept. It humorously points out that in life, unlike the dictionary, hustle must precede huge achievements. This is not just a play on words but a profound truth about the order of success. To achieve anything significant, you must first be willing to put in the work.

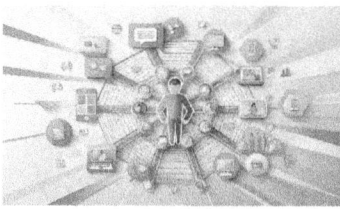

A roadmap to success involves recognizing that hustle and discipline are non-negotiable. It's about understanding that there are no shortcuts. Every overnight success story you've heard is the rest of the results from work that went unnoticed. The hustle is the groundwork that makes the eventual breakthrough possible.

Developing hustle and discipline starts with setting clear, achievable goals. Goals give your hustle direction and your discipline a purpose. Without goals, your efforts are scattered, and your discipline lacks focus. A well-defined goal is like a lighthouse guiding your hustle through the fog of daily distractions and setbacks.

Daily routines are the building blocks of discipline. Creating and sticking to a routine trains your mind to expect certain behaviors at specific times, making discipline almost automatic. It's like programming your brain to hustle without consciously thinking about it. Over time, these routines become the foundation of your success.

One common misconception is that hustle means constant work without rest. On the contrary, effective hustle includes strategic rest and recovery. Your body and mind need time to recharge to keep peak performance. This is where discipline also plays a crucial role, ensuring you balance work with adequate rest.

The beauty of hustle and discipline is that they are accessible to everyone. You don't need unique talents or unique CES; you need the willingness to work hard and the commitment to stay disciplined. This democratizes success, making it attainable for anyone willing to put in the effort.

Let's not forget the importance of resilience in keeping hustle and discipline. There will be setbacks, failures, and disappointments. Resilience is the ability to bounce back from these setbacks and continue hustling. It's about viewing failures as opportunities to learn and grow rather than reasons to quit.

Time management is another critical aspect. Hustling out proper time management can lead to burnout. Discipline helps you prioritize tasks and give time efficiently, ensuring you work smarter and not hardcore complicated. Balance prevents burnout and keeps your hustle sustainable in the long run.

Accountability partners can significantly boost your hustle and discipline. Having someone to check in with, share progress, and hold you accountable creates an external pressure that reinforces your internal discipline. It's like having a gym buddy who motivates you to show up even when you don't feel like it.

Visualizing success can also enhance your hustle. Seeing yourself achieving your goals can provide the motivation needed to keep hustling. Visualization works because it creates a mental picture of what you're working towards, making the effort feel more tangible and worthwhile.

Mindfulness and self-reflection are tools that can fine-tune your hustle and discipline. Regularly reflecting on your progress, understanding your motivations, and adjusting your strategies ensures that your hustle stays aligned with your goals. It's about being mindful of your journey and making necessary tweaks.

A positive attitude is crucial. Hustle with a negative mindset can feel like a burden. Discipline with a pessimistic outlook can be demotivating. Cultivating a positive attitude makes the hustle enjoyable and discipline rewarding. It transforms hard work from a chore into a passionate pursuit.

Networking is an often-overlooked aspect of hustle. Building connections and relationships can open doors that hard work alone might not. It's about using the power of your network to amplify your hustle. This doesn't mean relying on others but recognizing that success is often a team effort.

Self-care should be integrated into your hustle routine. Taking care of your physical and mental health ensures you have the energy and clarity to keep your hustle. Discipline includes knowing when to take a break and prioritize self-care without feeling guilty.

The role of mentors cannot be overstated. Someone has walked the path before and can provide invaluable guidance and inspiration. A mentor can help you avoid common pitfalls and accelerate your journey by sharing their experiences and wisdom.

Setting boundaries is part of a disciplined hustle. Knowing when to say no to distractions and yes to opportunities that align with your goals ensures that your hustle still is focused and effective.

Technology can be a powerful ally in your hustle. Utilizing productivity apps, time management tools and other digital resources can streamline your efforts and keep you organized. Technology can also automate repetitive tasks, freeing up more time for focused hustle.

Celebrate small wins. Recognizing and rewarding yourself for progress, no matter how minor, keeps your motivation high. It's a way of asking for our hard work and keeping the momentum needed for sustained discipline.

Continual learning is essential. The world is constantly evolving, which requires a commitment to education and self-improvement. This means regularly updating your skills and knowledge to remain competitive and practical.

Community support can provide a significant boost. Being part of a community of like-minded individuals who share your goals and values creates a supportive environment that nurtures your hustle and discipline. It's about finding your tribe that cheers you on.

Understanding your why is fundamental. Knowing why you hustle provides a deep-rooted motivation that keeps you going, even when the going gets tough. The fuel powers your discipline and keeps you focused on your goals.

Flexibility in your approach can enhance your hustle. While discipline provides the structure, flexibility allows you to adapt to changing circumstances without losing momentum. It's about being rigid in your goals but flexible in your methods.

The power of routine should not be underestimated. Routines create a rhythm that makes hustle automatic and discipline effortless. Over time, these routines become second nature, seamlessly integrating hustle into your daily life.

Gratitude can transform your hustle experience. 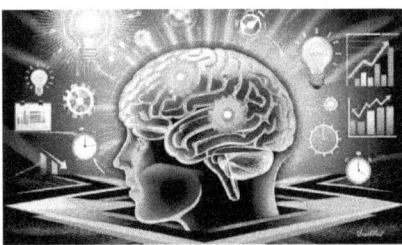 Focusing on what you have and what you've achieved fosters a positive mindset that makes the journey enjoyable. It's about appreciating the process as much as the outcome.

Publicly committing to your goals can strengthen your discipline. Sharing your goals with others creates a sense of accountability and increases your commitment to seeing them through. It's a psychological trick that makes your hustle more concrete.

In Summary, hustle and discipline are the twin pillars of success. They are not about relentless work, but about intelligent, consistent effort guided by clear goals and sustained by routines, self-care, and a positive mindset. Embrace hustle and discipline and watch as your dreams transform into reality.

Chapter 2: The Essence of Hustle – Why Hard Work Comes First

Hustle is more than just a buzzword; it's the backbone of every success story. Imagine a world-class athlete preparing for the Olympics. Their journey is characterized  by countless hours of training, pushing their limits, and refining their skills. This relentless hustle is what sets them apart and propels them to greatness. In the same way, any significant achievement in life or business demands this level of commitment and hard work.

At its core, hustle is about doing whatever it takes to achieve your goals. It's about showing up, doing the work, and staying committed even when the going gets tough. Hustle is the driving force that propels you send and the differentiator that sets successful people apart from the rest.

Consider the story of Sarah, an entrepreneur who started her business with nothing but a dream and a lot of hustle. She worked long hours, often sacrificing weekends and holidays. Her dedication paid off when her small startup grew into a thriving company. Sarah's story is a testament to the power of hustle and why hard work must always come first.

Natural talent can give you a head start, but hustle is what will get you to the finish line. It's easy to admire someone who seems naturally gifted, but without hustle, that talent often goes to waste. Hard work bridges the gap between where you are and where you want to be, ensuring your potential is fully realized.

The role of effort in success cannot be overstated. Those who put in the most effort is usually the most successful in any field. This effort often surpasses natural talent, proving a willingness to continually learn, grow, and improve. It's this relentless pursuit of excellence that leads to extraordinary achievements.

Hustle is not just about working hard; it's about working smart. It's about prioritizing tasks, managing time efficiently, and staying focused on your goals. Smart hustle involves using your resources wisely, seeking opportunities, and using your strengths to maximize productivity and results.

In professional contexts, hustle translates to going above and beyond the basic requirements of the job. It's about taking initiative, seeking out new challenges, and continually striving for excellence. This kind of dedication is what gets you noticed, earns you promotions, and accelerates your career growth.

On a personal level, hustle might mean investing time in self-improvement, pursuing hobbies, or developing new skills. It's about being proactive in all areas of life, not just work. This proactive attitude fosters a sense of accomplishment and fulfillment, contributing to overall happiness and success.

Academic hustle is equally important. Students who put in the extra effort to study, take part in class, and seek help when needed are the ones who excel. This academic hustle lays the groundwork for future success, teaching valuable lessons in discipline, time management, and perseverance.

Real-life examples abound of individuals who have achieved remarkable success through relentless hustle. Take the story of Thomas Edison, who famously said, "Genius is one percent inspiration and ninety-nine percent perspiration." Edison's relentless hustle and countless hours in the lab led to the invention of the light bulb and many other innovations that changed the world.

Another inspiring example is Oprah Winfrey, who overcame many obstacles through sheer hustle. From her early days in broadcasting to building a media empire, Oprah's journey is a powerful reminder that, combined with unwavering determination, it can lead to monumental success.

Hustle is often associated with sacrifice. It's about giving up short-term pleasures for long-term gains. This might mean working on a project instead of going out with friends or waking up early to fit in a workout before a busy day. These sacrifices, however, are what set the foundation for future success.

The rewards of hustle are not always immediate. Sometimes, it takes months or even years of consistent effort to see significant results. This delayed gratification can be challenging, but it also makes the eventual success all the more rewarding. Knowing your hard work paid off is incredibly fulfilling and motivates you to keep pushing forward.

One of the most significant benefits of hustle is the development of a strong work ethic. This work ethic becomes a part of your identity, influencing how you approach challenges and opportunities. It instills a sense of pride and accomplishment, knowing you can achieve anything you set your mind to through hard work.

Hustle also fosters resilience. The road to success is rarely smooth, and setbacks are inevitable. However, those who hustle learn to view these setbacks as temporary obstacles rather than insurmountable barriers. They develop the resilience to bounce back, learn from their mistakes, and keep moving forward.

Collaboration and hustle often go hand in hand. Working with others who share your drive and determination can amplify your efforts and lead to even greater success. It is more significant to create a supportive environment where everyone is motivated to give their best and work towards common goals.

Hustle is not just about the physical act of working hard; it also involves a mental part. Maintaining a positive and focused mindset is crucial for sustaining long-term hustle. It's about believing in yourself, staying motivated, and pushing through challenges with determination and optimism.

Self-discipline is a vital aspect of hustle. It's staying focused on your goals, even when distractions and temptations arise. This discipline ensures your efforts are consistent and aligned with your long-term aims, preventing you from veering off course.

The essence of hustle is rooted in passion. When you're passionate about what you do, your workplace becomes less of a chore and more of a joy. This passion fuels your drive, making the hard work worthwhile and motivating you through the ups and downs.

Hustle often leads to unexpected opportunities. When you work and stay dedicated, doors you didn't even know existed begin to open. These opportunities can propel you forward, taking your success to new heights and creating a ripple effect of positive outcomes.

In Summary, hustle is the foundation upon which success is built. It's about putting in the hard work, staying disciplined, and never giving up, even when faced with challenges. Hustle transforms dreams into reality with consistent effort and extraordinary achievements. Part 3: Developing Discipline - The Backbone of Consistent Success.

Chapter 3: Developing Discipline – The Backbone of Consistent Success

Discipline is the backbone of convenience. The steady, handy hand guides your hustle, ensuring that your  efforts are sustained over time. Even the most intense hustle can fizzle without discipline, leaving you short of your goals. Discipline keeps you going long after the first excitement has worn off, transforming hard work into lasting habits.

At its core, discipline is about self-control and the ability to delay gratification. It's about making choices that align with your long-term goals, even when those are difficult or inconvenient. Discipline means saying no to immediate pleasures in favor of future rewards, a concept that is easier said than done.

Developing discipline begins with setting clear, achievable goals. These goals provide direction and purpose, making it easier to stay focused and motivated. When you know what you're working towards, it's easier to make disciplined choices that support your journey.

Building solid habits is a crucial part of discipline. Habits are actions that become automatic through repetition, requiring less conscious effort over time. By developing habits that support your goals, you can make discipline a natural part of your routine. This might include habits like regular exercise, consistent study times, or daily planning sessions.

Time management is another essential aspect of discipline. Allocating your time effectively ensures you're working on the right tasks at the right time, maximizing your productivity. Tools like calendars, to-do lists, and time-blocking techniques can help you stay organized and focused.

Self-control is at the heart of discipline. It's the ability to resist temptations and distractions and stay committed to your goals. Developing self-control takes practice, but it can be strengthened over time, much like a muscle. Techniques like mindfulness, meditation, and visualization can help enhance self-control.

Setting boundaries is an essential part of keeping discipline. This means knowing when to say no to activities or commitments that don't align with your goals. Boundaries protect your time and energy, ensuring you stay focused on what matters most.

Accountability can significantly boost your discipline. Sharing your goals with others and having someone to check in with regularly creates a sense of responsibility. This external pressure can reinforce your internal discipline, helping you stay on track.

Practical techniques for building discipline include breaking tasks into smaller, manageable steps. This makes large projects feel less overwhelming and allows you to make steady progress. Each small step completed builds momentum, making it easier to stay disciplined.

Another effective strategy is creating routines. Routines set up a predictable pattern for your day, reducing the mental effort required to make decisions. By incorporating your goals into your daily routine, you can ensure that you're consistently working towards them without having to rely on willpower alone.

Monitoring your progress is crucial for keeping discipline. Regularly tracking your achievements helps you stay motivated and provides a sense of accomplishment. It also allows you to name areas where you may need to adjust your approach or redouble your efforts.

Celebrating small wins is an integral part of supporting discipline. Recognizing and rewarding yourself for progress, no matter how minor, keeps your motivation high. It acknowledges your hard work and supports the momentum for sustained discipline.

Building a support system can enhance your discipline. Surrounding yourself with like-minded individuals who share your goals and values creates a supportive environment. This community can offer encouragement, advice, and accountability, making it easier to stay disciplined.

Understanding your motivations is critical to critical discipline. Knowing why you want to achieve your goals provides a deep-rooted incentive to stay focused and committed. This intrinsic motivation is often more robust and sustainable than external rewards.

Flexibility in your approach can also support your discipline. While staying committed to your goals is essential, being too rigid can lead to burnout. Allowing yourself flexibility in achieving your goals can make the process more enjoyable and sustainable.

Practicing mindfulness can enhance your discipline by increasing your awareness of your thoughts and actions. Mindfulness helps you stay present and focused, making it easier to resist distractions and remain committed to your goals.

Visualizing your success can strengthen your discipline. Creating a mental picture of what you want to achieve makes your goals feel more tangible and achievable. This visualization can provide a powerful source of motivation and reinforce your commitment to disciplined action.

Building resilience is an essential part of keeping discipline. The journey to success is rarely smooth, and setbacks are inevitable. Resilience is the ability to bounce back from these setbacks, learn from them, and continue moving forward. It's about viewing challenges as opportunities for growth rather than reasons to give up.

Developing a growth mindset can enhance your discipline. A growth mindset is the belief that one can develop one's abilities and intelligence through hard work and dedication. This mindset encourages one to embrace challenges, persist through difficulties, and view failures as learning opportunities.

Discipline also involves taking care of your physical and mental health. Ensuring enough sleep, eating a balanced diet, and exercising regularly provide the energy and clarity needed to stay focused and productive. Self-care is a crucial part of sustained discipline.

Setting realistic and achievable goals is essential for keeping discipline. Too ambitious goals can lead to frustration and burnout, while goals that are too easy may not provide enough motivation. Finding the right balance ensures that your goals are challenging yet attainable.

Reflecting on your progress is an essential part of keeping discipline. Regularly reviewing your achievements, understanding your motivations, and adjusting your strategies ensures that your efforts are still aligned with your goals. It's about being mindful of your journey and making necessary tweaks.

Gratitude can transform your discipline experience. Focusing on what you have and what you've achieved fosters a positive mindset that makes the journey enjoyable. It's about appreciating the process as much as the outcome.

Publicly committing to your goals can strengthen your discipline. Sharing your goals with others creates a sense of accountability and increases your commitment to seeing them through. It's a psychological trick that makes your hustle more concrete.

In Summary, discipline is the backbone of consistent success. It's about developing solid habits, solving time effectively, and staying committed to your goals. By embracing discipline, you can ensure that your hustle is sustained over the long term, leading to lasting achievements and success.

Chapter 4: Turning on Your Natural Training – Leveraging Skills and Habits

Natural training refers to the skills, habits, and routines that you've developed over time, often without even realizing it.  These are the automatic actions and behaviors that come naturally to you and can be used to enhance your hustle and discipline. By recognizing and harnessing these natural tendencies, you can streamline your efforts and maximize your productivity.

Understanding your natural training begins with self-awareness. This involves taking a step back and analyzing your daily routines, finding the habits that support your goals, and recognizing the skills that come naturally to you. This self-awareness is the first step in using your natural training to achieve success.

Finding critical skills is crucial for turning on your natural training. These skills are the ones that you excel at and enjoy using. They could be anything from time management and organization to communication and problem-solving. Focusing on these strengths can enhance your hustle and make discipline feel more natural.

Once you've found your critical skills, the next step is to integrate them into your daily routines. This means structuring your day to allow you to use these skills regularly. For example, if you're naturally good at time management, you might create a detailed schedule outlining your tasks. This uses your strengths and ensures that you stay focused and productive.

Creating routines that align with your natural training can make hustle feel effortless. These routines become second nature, reducing the mental effort required to stay disciplined. Over time, they transform into habits that support your long-term goals.

Habit stacking is an effective technique for using your natural training. This involves pairing a new habit with an existing one, making it easier to adopt. For example, if you want to start meditating daily, you might stack this habit onto your existing morning coffee routine. This way, the new habit feels less like a disruption and more like a natural extension of your routine.

Activator training involves finding triggers that automatically activate your natural skills and habits. These triggers can include mental cues, specific times of day, or particular activities. For example, if you're more productive in the morning, you might schedule your most important tasks. This aligns your work with your natural rhythms, making hustle feel more effortless.

Leveraging your natural training also involves recognizing and minimizing activities that drain your energy or distract you from your goals. This might mean delegating tasks you you're doing or dropping unnecessary activities from your schedule. By focusing on what you do best, you can maximize your productivity and keep a high level of discretion, which is an ongoing process of turning on your natural traits. Regularly evaluating your routines and habits helps you stay aligned with your goals and make necessary adjustments. It's about being mindful of what's working and what's not and making tweaks to ensure continuous improvement.

Developing a growth mindset is crucial for using your natural training. This mindset encourages you to view challenges as opportunities to learn and grow. It's about believing that your abilities can be developed through hard work and dedication and continuously seeking improvement

Surrounding yourself with a supportive environment can enhance your natural training. This includes having a workspace that minimizes distractions, a network of like-minded individuals who support your goals, and tools that streamline your efforts. A supportive environment makes it easier to stay focused and disciplined.

Accountability partners can play a significant role in turning on your natural training. Having someone to check in with, share progress, and hold you accountable reinforces your discipline and enhances your hustle. It's like having a gym buddy who motivates you to show up and give your best.

Visualizing success can help activate your natural training. Creating a mental picture of what you want to achieve makes your goals feel more tangible and achievable. This visualization can provide a powerful source of motivation and reinforce your commitment to disciplined action.

Continuous learning is essential for maximizing your natural training. The world constantly evolves, and staying ahead requires a commitment to education and self-improvement. This means regularly updating your skills and knowledge to remain competitive and practical.

Building resilience is critical to supporting your natural training. The journey to success is rarely smooth, and setbacks are inevitable. Resilience is the ability to bounce back from these setbacks, learn from them, and continue moving forward. It's about viewing challenges as opportunities for growth rather than reasons to give up.

Gratitude can transform your natural training experience. Focusing on what you have and what you've achieved fosters a positive mindset that makes the journey enjoyable. It's about appreciating the process as much as the outcome.

Publicly committing to your goals can strengthen your natural training. Sharing your goals with others creates a sense of accountability and increases your commitment to seeing them through. It's a psychological trick that makes your hustle more concrete.

Flexibility in your approach can enhance your natural training. While discipline provides the structure, flexibility allows you to adapt to changing circumstances without losing momentum. It's about being rigid in your goals but flexible in your methods.

Celebrating small wins is an integral part of using your natural training. Recognizing and rewarding yourself for progress, no matter how minor, keeps your motivation high. It acknowledges and keeps the seed for sustained discipline.

In Summary, turning on your natural training involves recognizing and harnessing your skills, habits, and routines to enhance your hustle and discipline. By using your strengths and creating supportive environments, you can make hustle feel more effortless and achieve lasting success.

Chapter 5: Automating Discipline – Making Hard Work a Habit

Automating discipline is about creating systems and routines that make hard work a natural part of your daily. When  discipline becomes a habit, it requires less conscious effort, allowing you to focus your energy on achieving your goals. This chapter explores practical strategies for making discipline automatic, ensuring that your hustle is consistent and sustainable.

The power of automation lies in its ability to reduce the mental effort needed to stay disciplined. By proving routines and systems, you create a structure that supports your goals, making it easier to stay focused and productive. This automation transforms discipline from a conscious effort into a natural part of your daily life.

Creating routines is the first step in automating discipline. Routines prove a predictable pattern for your day, reducing the mental effort required to make decisions. By incorporating your goals into your daily routine, you can ensure that you're consistently working towards them without having to rely on willpower alone.

Time-blocking is an effective technique for creating routines. It involves scheduling specific blocks of time for different tasks, ensuring that you distribute enough time for important activities. Time-blocking helps you stay organized and focused, making it easier to keep discipline.

Habit tracking is another powerful tool for automating discipline. By tracking your habits, you can check your progress and stay motivated. Habit-tracking apps and journals can help you stay accountable and ensure that you're consistently working towards your goals.

Building micro-habits is a practical strategy for automating discipline. Micro-habits are small, manageable actions that contribute to your larger goals. Starting with small, achievable habits can build momentum and gradually increase your efforts, making discipline feel less overwhelming and more attainable.

Environmental design plays a crucial role in automating discipline. Creating a supportive environment that minimizes distractions and maximizes productivity can enhance discipline. This might involve organizing your workspace, setting up reminders, or making a designated area for focused work.

Accountability partners can help automate discipline by providing external motivation and support. Having someone to check in with regularly creates a sense of responsibility and reinforces your commitment to your goals. This accountability can make it easier to stay disciplined and keep consistent effort.

Self-reflection is an essential part of automating discipline. Regularly evaluating your routines and habits helps you stay aligned with your goals and make necessary adjustments. It's about being mindful of what's working and what's not and making tweaks to ensure continuous improvement.

Visualizing success can strengthen your discipline. Creating a mental picture of what you want to achieve makes your goals feel more tangible and achievable. This visualization can provide a powerful source of motivation and reinforce your commitment to disciplined action.

Continuous learning is essential for keeping automated discipline. The world constantly evolves, and staying ahead requires a commitment to education and self-improvement. This means regularly updating your skills and knowledge to remain competitive and practical.

Building resilience is critical to supporting automated discipline. The journey to success is rarely smooth, and setbacks are inevitable. Resilience is the ability to bounce back from these setbacks, learn from them, and continue moving forward. It's about viewing challenges as opportunities for growth rather than reasons to give up.

Gratitude can transform your discipline experience. Focusing on what you have and what you've achieved fosters a positive mindset that makes the journey enjoyable. It's about appreciating the process as much as the outcome.

Publicly committing to your goals can strengthen your discipline. Sharing your goals with others creates a sense of accountability and increases your commitment to seeing them through. It's a psychological trick that makes your hustle more concrete.

Flexibility in your approach can enhance your natural training. While discipline provides the structure, flexibility allows you to adapt to changing circumstances without losing momentum. It's about being rigid in your goals but flexible in your methods.

Celebrating small wins is an integral part of keeping automated discipline. Recognizing and rewarding yourself for progress, no matter how minor, keeps your motivation high. It acknowledges hard work and supports the momentum needed for sustained discipline.

In Summary, automating discipline is about creating systems and routines that make hard work a natural part of daily life. By showing and using tools and techniques and building resilience, you can make discipline feel effortless and achieve lasting success.

Chapter 6: Overcoming Obstacles – Staying Motivated and Focused

Obstacles are an inevitable part of the journey to success, but how you handle them can make all the difference. Staying motivated and focused in the face of challenges requires a combination of strategies, mindset shifts, and practical tools. This chapter explores overcoming common obstacles and keeping the drive needed to achieve your goals.

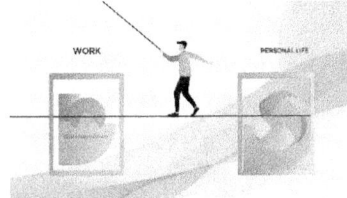

One of the most common obstacles is procrastination. It's easy to delay tasks, especially those that seem daunting or unpleasant.

. To overcome procrastination, break tasks into smaller, more manageable steps. This makes them feel less overwhelmed and allows them to make steady progress. Setting deadlines for each step can also create a sense of urgency and help you stay on track.

Burnout is another significant obstacle. When you push yourself too hard without adequate rest, it can lead to physical and mental exhaustion. Preventing burnout requires balancing work with rest and self-care. This might involve scheduling regular breaks, setting realistic goals, and engaging in activities that recharge your energy.

Distractions are everywhere in our modern world, from social media to household chores. To stay focused, create a distraction-free environment. This might involve setting up a dedicated workspace, using apps that block distracting websites, or proving specific times for focused work. Minimizing distractions allows you to concentrate fully on your tasks.

Maintaining motivation over the long term can be challenging, especially when progress seems slow. One strategy is to set small, achievable goals that lead to a larger goal. Celebrating these small wins provides a sense of accomplishment and keeps your motivation high. It's about recognizing and rewarding yourself for the effort, not just the outcome.

Staying motivated also involves connecting with your why. Understanding the deeper reasons behind your goals provides a powerful source of motivation. When you know why you're working hard, it's easier to stay committed, even when the going gets tough. This intrinsic motivation is often more sustainable than external rewards.

Building a support system can significantly boost your motivation and focus. Surrounding yourself with like-minded individuals who share your goals and values creates a supportive environment. This community can offer encouragement, advice, and accountability, making staying motivated and on track easier.

Visualization is a powerful tool for keeping focus. Creating a mental picture of your goals and the steps needed to achieve them makes the process feel more tangible and achievable. Visualization can also provide inspiration and motivation, helping you stay focused on your aims.

Resilience is critical to overcritical obstacles. The journey to success is rarely smooth, and setbacks are inevitable. Resilience is the ability to bounce back from these setbacks, learn from them, and continue moving forward. It's about viewing challenges as opportunities for growth rather than reasons to give up.

Self-reflection is essential for keeping motivation and focus. Regularly reviewing your progress, understanding your motivations, and adjusting your strategies ensures that your efforts are still aligned with your goals. It's about being mindful of your journey and making necessary tweaks.

Flexibility in your approach can enhance your ability to overcome obstacles. While discipline provides the structure, flexibility allows you to adapt to changing circumstances without losing momentum. It's about being rigid in your goals but flexible in your methods.

Mindfulness can help you stay focused and motivated. Practicing mindfulness increases your awareness of your thoughts and actions, making it easier to resist distractions and remain committed to your goals. Mindfulness techniques like meditation, deep breathing, and journaling can enhance focus and clarity.

Accountability partners can play a significant role in overcoming obstacles. Having someone to check in with regularly creates a sense of responsibility and reinforces your commitment to your goals. This accountability can make it easier to stay disciplined and keep consistent effort.

Continuous learning is essential for overcoming obstacles. The world constantly evolves, and staying ahead requires a commitment to education and self-improvement. This means regularly updating your skills and knowledge to remain competitive and practical in your hustle.

Gratitude can transform your experience of overcoming obstacles. Focusing on what you have and what you've achieved fosters a positive mindset that makes the journey enjoyable. It's about appreciating the process as much as the outcome.

Publicly committing to your goals can strengthen your motivation and focus. Sharing your goals with others creates a sense of accountability and increases your commitment to seeing them through. It's a psychological trick that makes your hustle more concrete.

Celebrating small wins is an integral part of keeping motivation and focus. Recognizing and rewarding yourself for progress, no matter how minor, keeps your motivation high. It acknowledges your hard work and keeps the momentum needed for sustained discipline.

In Summary, overcoming obstacles requires a combination of strategies, mindset shifts, and practical tools. By creating supportive environments, using tools and techniques, and building resilience, you can stay motivated and focused and achieve your goals.

Chapter 7: Measuring Progress – Tracking Your Journey to Success

Tracking your progress is essential for staying motivated and adjusting your strategies. By measuring your achievements and naming areas for  improvement, you can ensure that your efforts are aligned with your goals. This chapter explores effective practices for tracking progress and analyzing your journey to success.

The importance of tracking progress cannot be overstated. It provides a clear picture of where and how far you've come, helping you stay motivated and focused. Tracking progress also allows you to show what's working and what's not, enabling you to make necessary adjustments to your approach.

Effective tracking methods begin with setting clear, measurable goals. These goals should be specific, attainable, and time-bound, providing a clear roadmap for your efforts. By breaking down your goals into smaller, manageable tasks, you can track your progress more accurately and stay on track.

Journaling is a powerful tool for tracking progress. By regularly creating a detailed record of your journey by documenting your thoughts, actions, and achievements, you can reflect on your experiences, find patterns, and gain insights into your progress. Journaling also provides a sense of accountability, making staying committed to your goals easier.

Progress charts are another effective tracking method. Visualizing your progress through charts or graphs provides a clear, tangible representation of your achievements. This visual feedback can be highly motivating, encouraging you to keep pushing forward.

Digital tools and apps can streamline the process of tracking progress. From project management software to habit-tracking apps, these tools offer a convenient way to check your efforts and stay organized. Many apps offer features like reminders, progress reports, and goal-setting templates, making it easier to stay on track.

Analyzing your progress is a crucial part of the tracking process. Regularly reviewing your achievements and finding areas for improvement ensures that your efforts are still aligned with your goals. This analysis involves looking at quantitative and qualitative data, from metrics and numbers to personal reflections and insights.

Self-reflection is an essential way of analyzing progress. Reflecting on your experiences, understanding your motivations, and adjusting your strategies ensures that your efforts stay focused and effective. Self-reflection helps you stay mindful of your journey and make necessary tweaks.

Continuous learning is essential for effective progress tracking. The world constantly evolves, and staying ahead requires a commitment to education and self-improvement. This means regularly updating your skills and knowledge to remain competitive and practical in your hustle.

Accountability partners can enhance your progress tracking. Having someone to check in with regularly creates a sense of responsibility and reinforces your commitment to your goals. This accountability can provide valuable feedback and support, helping you stay on track and make necessary adjustments.

Gratitude can transform your experience of tracking progress. Focusing on what you have and what you've achieved fosters a positive mindset that makes the journey enjoyable. It's about appreciating the process as much as the outcome.

Publicly committing to your goals can strengthen your progress tracking. Sharing your goals with others creates a sense of accountability and increases your commitment to seeing them through. It's a psychological trick that makes your hustle more concrete.

Celebrating small wins is an integral part of tracking progress. Recognizing and rewarding yourself for progress, no matter how minor, keeps your motivation high. It acknowledges your hard work and supports the momentum needed for sustained discipline.

Flexibility in your approach can enhance your progress tracking. While discipline provides the structure, flexibility allows you to adapt to changing circumstances without losing momentum. It's about being rigid in your goals but flexible in your methods.

Building resilience is key to supporting automated discipline. The journey to success is rarely smooth, and setbacks are inevitable. Resilience is the ability to bounce back from these setbacks, learn from them, and continue moving forward. It's about viewing challenges as opportunities for growth rather than reasons to give up.

Visualizing success can strengthen your progress tracking. Creating a mental picture of what you want to achieve makes your goals feel more tangible and achievable. This visualization can provide a powerful source of motivation and reinforce your commitment to disciplined action.

Continuous improvement is essential for effective progress tracking. Regularly evaluating your routines and habits helps you stay aligned with your goals and make necessary adjustments. It's about being mindful of what's working and what's not and making tweaks to ensure continuous improvement.

In Summary, tracking your progress is essential for staying motivated and adjusting your strategies. By setting clear goals, using effective tracking methods, and regularly analyzing your achievements, you can ensure that your efforts align with your goals and that you're on the path to success.

Chapter 8: Continuous Improvement – Enhancing Your Skills and Habits

Continuous improvement is the key to sustained success. By regularly enhancing your skills and habits, you can stay competitive and achieve excellent scores  in time. This chapter explores the importance of continuous improvement and provides strategies for incorporating it into your daily routine.

The need for continuous improvement is driven by the world's constantly evolving nature. New technologies, changing markets, and emerging trends require you to stay adaptable and continually update your skills and knowledge. Continuous improvement ensures that you are still relevant and practical in your hustle.

Showing areas for growth is the first step in continuous improvement. This involves regularly evaluating your skills and habits, naming strengths and weaknesses, and setting goals for development. Self-awareness is crucial in this process, allowing you to focus on the areas with the most significant impact.

Seeking feedback is an integral part of finding areas for growth. Feedback from mentors, peers, and colleagues offers valuable insights into your performance and helps you find blind spots. Constructive feedback can highlight improvement areas and guide you in enhancing your skills and habits.

Setting higher goals is a powerful strategy for continuous improvement.

Once you've achieved a goal, setting a new, more challenging one ensures that you continue to grow and develop. These higher goals push you out of your comfort zone and encourage you to strive for excellence.

Learning new skills is a crucial part of continuous improvement. This might involve taking courses, attending workshops, reading books, or seeking new experiences. By regularly expanding your skill set, you can stay ahead of the curve and enhance your ability to achieve your goals.

Implementing continuous improvement into your daily routine involves creating habits that support your growth. These might include dedicating time to learning, seeking new challenges, and regularly reviewing your progress. These habits ensure that continuous improvement becomes a natural part of your hustle.

Mindfulness and self-reflection are essential tools for continuous improvement. Regularly reflecting on your experiences, understanding your motivations, and adjusting your strategies ensures that your efforts stay aligned with your goals. It's about being mindful of your journey and making necessary tweaks.

Accountability partners can enhance your continuous improvement efforts. Having someone to check in with regularly creates a sense of responsibility and reinforces your commitment to your goals. This accountability provides valuable feedback and support, helping you stay on track and make necessary adjustments.

Gratitude can transform your experience of continuous improvement. Focusing on what you have and what you've achieved fosters a positive mindset that makes the journey enjoyable. It's about appreciating the process as much as the outcome.

Publicly committing to your goals can strengthen your continuous improvement efforts. Sharing your goals with others creates a sense of accountability and increases your commitment to seeing them through. It's a psychological trick that makes your hustle more concrete.

Celebrating small wins is an important part of continuous movement. Recognizing and rewarding yourself for progress, no matter how minor, keeps your motivation high. It acknowledges hard work and keeps the momentum needed for sustained discipline.

Flexibility in your approach can enhance your continuous improvement efforts. While discipline provides the structure, flexibility allows you to adapt to changing circumstances without losing momentum. It's about being rigid in your goals but flexible in your methods.

Building resilience is critical to continuous improvement. The journey to success is rarely smooth, and setbacks are inevitable. Resilience is the ability to bounce back from these setbacks, learn from them, and continue moving forward. It's about viewing challenges as opportunities for growth rather than reasons to give up.

Visualizing success can strengthen your continuous improvement efforts. Creating a mental picture of what you want to achieve makes your goals feel more tangible and achievable. This visualization can provide a powerful source of motivation and reinforce your commitment to disciplined action.

Continuous learning is essential for effective continuous improvement. The world constantly evolves, and staying ahead requires a commitment to education and self-improvement. This means regularly updating your skills and knowledge to remain competitive and practical in your hustle.

In Summary, continuous improvement is the key to sustained success. By regularly enhancing your skills and habits, you can stay competitive and achieve tremendous success over time. By finding areas for growth, seeking feedback, and setting higher goals, you can ensure that continuous improvement becomes a natural part of your daily routine.

Chapter 9: Real-Life Success Stories – Learning from the Best

Inspirational success stories can provide valuable insights and motivation. By learning from the experiences of others, you can gain practical strategies  and inspiration to apply to your own journey. This chapter explores real-life success stories and highlights the lessons learned from these individuals' journeys.

One of the most inspiring success stories is that of Steve Jobs. Jobs co-founded Apple Inc. in his garage, and through relentless hustle and visionary leadership, he built it into one of the world's most valuable companies. Job's story is a testament to the power of perseverance, innovation, and the willingness to take risks. His journey teaches us the importance of staying true to our vision and continuously striving for excellence.

Another remarkable success story is that of Oprah Winfrey. Despite facing many challenges and setbacks, Oprah's unwavering determination and commitment to her goals propelled her to become one of the most influential media personalities in the world. Oprah's journey highlights the importance of resilience, self-belief, and the power of giving back to the community.

Elon Musk is another example of relentless hustle and innovation. From co-founding PayPal to leading companies like Tesla and SpaceX, Musk's journey is marked by his bold vision and tireless work ethic. His story underscores the importance of thinking big, taking calculated risks, and continuously pushing the boundaries of what's possible.

J.K. Rowling's story is a powerful reminder of the impact of perseverance and belief in oneself. Despite many rejections from publishers, Rowling's determination to bring the Harry Potter series to life eventually led to one of the most successful book franchises in history. Her journey teaches us the importance of persistence, creativity, and the power of storytelling.

The story of Richard Branson, founder of the Virgin Group, is a lesson in entrepreneurship and adaptability. Branson's willingness to explore new ventures and his fearless approach to business led to a global empire. His journey highlights the importance of curiosity, innovation, and the willingness to embrace failure as a learning opportunity.

Learning from these success stories involves finding the common traits and strategies contributing to their achievements. One common trait is an unwavering commitment to their goals, even in the face of obstacles. These individuals prove that success requires persistence, resilience, and a willingness to learn from failures.

Another key lesson from these stories is the importance of innovation and continuous improvement. Whether developing new products, exploring new markets, or improving existing processes, innovation plays a crucial role in achieving and sustaining success. These stories show that staying ahead of the curve requires a commitment to learning and adapting to changing circumstances.

Networking and building relationships are also crucial aspects of success. Many of these individuals achieved their goals by surrounding themselves with supportive networks of mentors, colleagues, and collaborators. This highlights the importance of building strong relationships and using the power of your network to achieve your goals.

The role of self-belief and confidence cannot be overstated. These success stories show that believing in yourself and your vision is essential for overcoming challenges and achieving your goals. Confidence provides the motivation and drive needed to overcome acks.

Taking calculated risks is another common theme in these success stories. Whether investing in an adventure, exploring uncharted territories, or making bold decisions, taking risks is often necessary for achieving significant success. These stories show that while risks can lead to failure, they also provide opportunities for growth and innovation.

Another important lesson is the value of giving back and contributing to the community. Many individuals have used their success to positively affect philanthropy, mentorship, or social initiatives. This highlights the importance of using your success to create a positive ripple effect and make a difference in the lives of others.

These stories clearly prove the importance of resilience. Successful individuals own the ability to bounce back from setbacks, learn from failures, and keep moving forward. Resilience ensures that one stays committed to one's goals, even when faced with challenges and obstacles.

Learning from these success stories also involves understanding the importance of self-care and work-life balance. While hustle and hard work are essential, it's also important to prioritize self-care and support a healthy balance. This ensures you have the energy and clarity to stay focused and productive.

In conclusion, real-life success stories provide valuable lessons and inspiration for your own journey. By naming the common traits and strategies that contributed to these individuals' achievements, you can gain practical insights and motivation to apply to your own hustle. Whether it's through perseverance, innovation, networking, or resilience, these stories highlight the importance of staying committed to your goals and continuously striving for excellence.

Chapter 10: Sustaining Long-Term Success Through Continuous Hustle and Learning

Sustaining long-term success requires a commitment to continuous hustle and learning. By consistently putting  in the effort and continually updating your skills and knowledge, you can achieve and support success over the long term. This chapter explores strategies for sustaining long-term success through continuous hustle and learning.

Adopting a growth mindset is the foundation of long-term success. This mindset involves viewing challenges and failures as opportunities to learn and grow. It's about believing that abilities can be developed through hard work and dedication. This mindset encourages continuous learning and improvement, ensuring that you stay ahead of the curve.

Continuing education is crucial for sustaining long-term success. This might involve formal education, professional development courses, or self-study. By regularly updating your skills and knowledge, you can stay relevant and effective in your hustle. Continuing education ensures that you stay competitive and able to adapt to changing circumstances.

Staying curious is another important aspect of learning. Curiosity drives you to explore new ideas, seek new experiences, and constantly improve your skills. It ensures that you are still engaged and motivated, making it easier to sustain long-term success.

Consistency over intensity is critical to sustaining long-term success. While short bursts of intense effort can lead to quick wins, consistent, sustained effort leads to lasting achievements. Consistency ensures that you stay focused on your goals and keep the momentum needed for long-term success.

Setting new goals is crucial for keeping motivation and drive. Once you've achieved a goal, setting a new, more challenging one ensures that you continue to grow and develop. These new goals push you out of your comfort zone and encourage you to strive for excellence.

Regular self-assessment is essential for sustainable long-term success. Regularly evaluating your progress and finding areas for improvement ensures that your efforts stay aligned with your goals. Self-assessment helps you stay mindful of your journey and make necessary tweaks.

Building a support system is essential for sustaining long-term success. Surrounding yourself with like-minded individuals who share your goals and values creates a supportive environment. This community can offer encouragement, advice, and accountability, making it easier to stay on track.

Finding men quickly can provide valuable guidance and support. Mentors can offer insights based on their own experiences to help you.

Navigate challenges and make informed decisions. Having a mentor can accelerate your growth and enhance your ability to achieve long-term success.

Creating a network of accountability partners can also enhance your efforts. Having someone to check in with regularly sets up a sense of responsibility and reinforces your commitment to your goals. This accountability can provide valuable feedback and support, helping you stay on track and make necessary adjustments.

Embracing change and adaptability is crucial for sustaining long-term success. The world is constantly evolving, and staying ahead requires a willingness to adapt to changing circumstances. Embracing change ensures that you are still flexible and open to new opportunities, making it easier to sustain your success.

Continuous innovation is another critical aspect of long-term success. Innovation is crucial to staying ahead, whether developing new products, exploring new markets, or improving existing processes. Continuous innovation ensures that you stay competitive and able to adapt to changing circumstances.

Learning from the competition can offer valuable insights. Studying your competitors' successes and mistakes can help you find opportunities for improvement and innovation. Learning from the competition ensures you stay ahead and continually enhance your efforts.

Celebrating milestones is an important part of sustaining long-term success. Recognizing and rewarding yourself for progress, no matter how minor, keeps your motivation high. It acknowledges your hard work and keeps the momentum for sustained discipline.

Reflecting on your journey is crucial for keeping motivation and focus. Taking time to reflect on your experiences, understand your motivations, and adjust your strategies ensures that your efforts align with your Reflection. This helps you stay mindful of your journey and make necessary tweaks.

Reevaluating goals regularly ensures that they stay aligned with your personal and professional aspirations. Periodically reassessing your goals and making necessary adjustments ensures that they continue to motivate and challenge you. This regular reevaluation ensures that your goals stay relevant and attainable.

A positive attitude is crucial for sustaining long-term success. Hustling with a negative mindset can feel like a burden, and discipline with a pessimistic outlook can be demotivating. Cultivating a positive attitude makes the hustle enjoyable and discipline rewarding. It transforms hard work from a chore into a passionate pursuit.

Networking is an often-overlooked aspect of hustle. Building connections and relationships can open doors that hard work alone might not. It's about using the power of your network to amplify your hustle. This doesn't mean relying on others but recognizing that success is often a team effort.

Self-care should be integrated into your hustle routine. Taking care of your physical and mental health ensures you have the energy and clarity to keep your hustle. Discipline includes knowing when to take a break and prioritize self-care without feeling guilty.

The role of mentors cannot be overstated. Someone has walked the path before and can provide invaluable guidance and inspiration. A mentor can help you avoid common pitfalls and accelerate your journey by sharing their experiences and wisdom.

Setting boundaries is part of a disciplined hustle. Knowing when to say no to distractions and yes to opportunities that align with your goals ensures that your hustle still is focused and effective.

Technology can be a powerful ally in your hustle. Utilizing productivity apps, time management tools and other digital resources can streamline your efforts and keep you organized. Technology can also automate repetitive tasks, freeing up more time for focused hustle.

In Summary, sustaining long-term success requires a commitment to continuous hustle and learning. By adopting a growth mindset, staying curious, and regularly updating your skills, you can ensure that you are motivated and effective in your efforts. Practically, adaptability and resilience are vital to supporting the drive and focus needed for long-term success.

Chapter 11: Huge Only Comes Before Hustle in the Dictionary

"Huge Only Comes Before Hustle in the Dictionary" is more than just a clever play on words; it's a profound commentary on  the nature of success and hard work. This saying emphasizes that while "huge" may precede "hustle" in the dictionary, in real life, significant achievements always come after sustained effort and dedication. Let's dive deeper into this concept and its implications for achieving success.

Firstly, it's essential to know the literal truth of the phrase. In the dictionary, the word "huge" indeed comes before "hustle" due to alphabetical order. This is purely technical and has no bearing on the real-world dynamics of success. The dictionary arranges words based on letters, not on the principles of achievement or effort. However, hustle — assertive, forceful, and focused action — is the prerequisite for achieving anything huge in life's journey.

Consider the world of sports. Athletes who win gold medals at the Olympics or break world records didn't just wake up one day and find themselves at the top. Their success results from years of grueling training, relentless practice, and an unwavering commitment to their goals. Their "huge" accomplishments are the fruits of their "hustle." The order of words in the dictionary might mislead one to think otherwise, but real life requires hustle before anything huge can be reached.

The significance of this phrase lies in its reminder that effort must precede reward. The dictionary order is a superficial arrangement that doesn't reflect the deeper, more meaningful truth about success. Success is built on a foundation of hard work, perseverance, and discipline. No one achieves greatness without first putting in the effort, often in the face of adversity and challenges.

Let's take a look at the story of J.K. Rowling. Before becoming a globally celebrated author with the Harry Potter series, Rowling faced many rejections from publishers. Her journey to "huge" success was paved with persistent hustle. She kept writing, editing, and giving her work despite the setbacks. The huge success of her books came only after she proved relentless hustle.

This phrase also serves as a motivational reminder. It tells us that if we aspire to achieve something massive, we must be prepared to hustle. It's a call to action, urging us to roll our sleeves and work. The dictionary may place "huge" before "hustle," but our lives should follow the opposite order.

In professional settings, this principle is clear. Take the example of a young entrepreneur. Building a successful business from the ground up requires more than just a good idea. It demands countless hours of market research, networking, product development, and marketing. The entrepreneur's huge success in creating a profitable company only comes after extensive hustle.

Similarly, in academics, students who achieve top grades or earn prestigious scholarships do so through dedicated study and hard work. Their achievements result from consistent effort, time management, and self-discipline. They achieve considerable milestones in their academic careers through relentless hustle.

The phrase also highlights the importance of resilience. Setbacks and failures are inevitable on the path to achieving something huge. Hustle involves more than just working hard; it involves bouncing back from disappointments and persisting despite obstacles. Resilience is a critical part of hustle that enables long-term success.

It's worth noting that hustle should not be equated with mere busyness. Effective hustle involves focus and strategy toward clear goals. It's about working smarter, not just more complicated. The dictionary order might place huge before hustle, but strategy leads to substantial achievements in practice.

The concept can also be applied to personal development. Personal growth and self-improvement require effort and dedication. Whether developing a new skill, improving physical fitness, or cultivating a positive mindset, the vast benefits of personal development are realized through consistent hustle.

Networking is another area where this principle applies. Building a solid professional network can lead to substantial career opportunities. However, this doesn't happen overnight. It requires consistent effort in building relationships, attending events, and providing value to others. The hustle of networking precedes the vast opportunities that come from it.

Moreover, the phrase underscores the importance of setting realistic expectations. It reminds us that colossal success doesn't come instantly. It takes time, patience, and persistent effort. Understanding this helps manage expectations and encourages a long-term perspective on success.

In Summary, "Huge Only Comes Before Hustle in the Dictionary" reminds us that real-life success requires hard work, persistence, and strategic effort. The dictionary order is superficial, but in the journey of life, hustle must always precede huge achievements. By embracing this principle, we can stay motivated, focused, and committed to our goals, knowing that our hustle will eventually lead to significant success.

Chapter 12: How to Automatically Turn on Your Natural Training and Discipline to Succeed

Turning on your natural training and discipline to succeed involves using the skills and habits you've developed to achieve your goals effortlessly. This chapter explores strategies for making discipline and hard work automatic, ensuring that your efforts are consistent and sustainable.

The concept of natural training refers to the skills, habits, and routines that you've honed over the years, often without even realizing it. These automatic behaviors can be powerful tools in your journey to success. By finding and using these natural tendencies, you can streamline your efforts and enhance your productivity.

Self-awareness is the first step in turning on your natural training. This involves taking a step back and analyzing your daily routines, finding the habits that support your goals, and recognizing the skills that come naturally to you. This self-awareness is crucial for using your natural training to achieve success.

Once you've named your critical skills and habits, the next step is to integrate them into your daily routines. Structuring your day to allow you to use these skills regularly can make discipline feel more natural. For example, if you're naturally good at time management, creating a detailed schedule that outlines your daily tasks can help you stay focused and productive.

Habit stacking is an effective technique for using your natural training. This involves pairing a new habit with an existing one, making it easier to adopt. For example, if you want to start meditating daily, you might stack this habit onto your existing morning coffee routine. This way, the new habit feels less like a disruption and more like a natural extension of your routine.

Creating routines that align with your natural training can make hustle feel effortless. These routines become second nature, reducing the mental effort required to stay disciplined. Over time, they transform into habits that support your long-term goals.

Activator training involves finding triggers that automatically activate your natural skills and habits. These triggers can include mental cues, specific times of day, or particular activities. For example, if you're more productive in the morning, you might schedule your most important tasks. This aligns your work with your natural rhythms, making hustle feel more effortless.

Leveraging your natural training also involves recognizing and minimizing activities that drain your energy or distract you from your goals. This might mean delegating tasks you're nodding and cutting unnecessary activities from your schedule. By focusing on what you do best, you can maximize your productivity and keep high discipline.

Self-reflection is an ongoing process of turning off your natural training. Regularly evaluating your routines and habits helps you stay aligned with your goals and make necessary adjustments. It's about being mindful of what's working and what's not and making tweaks to ensure continuous improvement.

Developing a growth mindset is crucial for using your natural training. This mindset encourages you to view challenges as opportunities to learn and grow. It's about believing that your abilities can be developed through hard work and dedication and continuously seeking improvement

Surrounding yourself with a supportive environment can enhance your natural training. This includes having a workspace that minimizes distractions, a network of like-minded individuals who support your goals, and tools that streamline your efforts. A supportive environment makes it easier to stay focused and disciplined.

Accountability partners can play a significant role in turning on your natural training. Having someone to check in with, share progress, and hold you accountable reinforces your discipline and enhances your hustle. It's like having a gym buddy who motivates you to show up and give your best.

Visualizing success can help activate your natural training. Creating a mental picture of what you want to achieve makes your goals feel more tangible and achievable. This visualization can provide a powerful source of motivation and reinforce your commitment to disciplined action.

Continuous learning is essential for maximizing your natural training. The world constantly evolves, and staying ahead requires a commitment to education and self-improvement. This means regularly updating your skills and knowledge to remain competitive and practical in your hustle.

Building resilience is critical to keeping your natural training. The journey to success is rarely smooth, and setbacks are inevitable. Resilience is the ability to bounce back from these setbacks, learn from them, and continue moving forward. It's about viewing challenges as opportunities for growth rather than reasons to give up.

Gratitude can transform your natural training experience. Focusing on what you have and what you've achieved fosters a positive mindset that makes the journey enjoyable. It's about appreciating the process as much as the outcome.

Publicly committing to your goals can strengthen your natural training. Sharing your goals with others creates a sense of accountability and increases your commitment to seeing them through. It's a psychological trick that makes your hustle more concrete.

Flexibility in your approach can enhance your natural training. While discipline provides the structure, flexibility allows you to adapt to changing circumstances without losing momentum. It's about being rigid in your goals but flexible in your methods.

Celebrating small wins is an integral part of using your natural training. Recognizing and rewarding yourself for progress, no matter how minor, keeps your motivation high. It acknowledges your hard work and keeps the momentum needed for sustained discipline.

In Summary, turning on your natural training involves recognizing and harnessing your skills, habits, and  routines to enhance your hustle and discipline. By using your strengths and creating supportive environments, you can make hustle feel more effortless and achieve lasting success.

Conclusion: Huge Success, Hustle Required: Unlock Your Natural Discipline

As we draw to a close, let's recap and reinforce the core message of this book: "Huge Only Comes Before Hustle in the Dictionary: How to Automatically Turn on Your Natural Training and Discipline to Succeed." Throughout the chapters, we've explored how hustle and discipline are not just essential, but fundamental, to achieving long-term success.  This conclusion aims to synthesize these ideas, leaving you with a clear understanding and a powerful call to action to integrate these principles into your life.

Recap of Key Concepts

The journey to success is paved with consistent hard work, dedication, and the relentless pursuit of improvement. Hustle is about doing whatever it takes to reach your goals, going the extra mile, and putting in the effort daily. Discipline is about keeping that effort consistently, even when motivation wanes. Together, they form the backbone of significant achievements.

We've emphasized that hustle and discipline are accessible to everyone. You don't need to be extraordinarily talented or lucky to succeed; you need the willingness to work hard and stay committed. This democratizes success, making it achievable for anyone willing to put in the effort.

The Value of Continuous Learning

Continuous learning is a crucial aspect of supporting hustle and discipline. The world constantly changes, and staying ahead requires a commitment to learning and self-improvement. This means regularly updating your skills, seeking new knowledge, and staying curious. Lifelong learning ensures you are still competitive and adaptable, ready to seize new opportunities.

We discussed the importance of a growth mindset, which involves viewing challenges as opportunities for growth and believing that your abilities can be developed through hard work and dedication. This mindset encourages you to embrace continuous learning and improvement, ensuring that you stay off the curve.

Outworking and Out-Learning

The combination of outworking and out-learning your competition is a powerful strategy for success. By putting in more effort and continually updating your skills, you can surpass those who rely solely on talent or luck. This approach ensures that you stay competitive and effective in your efforts, consistently achieving your goals.

Outworking involves supporting a high level of effort and dedication, going above and beyond the basic requirements. Out-learning involves seeking new knowledge and skills, staying curious, and continually improving. Together, these strategies create a formidable approach to achieving long-term success.

The Paradoxes of Persistence

The journey to success is filled with paradoxes that require a delicate balance. One such paradox is the need to balance patience with urgency. While staying patient and trusting the process is essential, it's equally important to keep a sense of urgency and consistently push forward.

Another paradox is the balance between consistency and flexibility. Consistency in your efforts ensures that you stay focused and make steady progress, while flexibility allows you to adapt to changing circumstances and seize new opportunities. Finding this balance is critical to sustaining long-term success.

Personal Insights and Reflections

Throughout this book, I've shared many stories and examples to illustrate the principles of hustle and discipline. These stories highlight the importance of perseverance, resilience, and the willingness to learn from failures. They prove that success is a journey, not a destination, and that consistent effort and dedication are essential.

Reflecting on my own journey, I can attest to the power of hustle and continuous learning. Every achievement I've experienced has been the result of hard work, discipline, and the relentless pursuit of improvement. These principles have transformed my life, and I hope they will do the same for you.

Practical Solutions for Overcoming Challenges

Challenges are an inevitable part of the journey to success. Common obstacles include procrastination, burnout, and distractions. We've discussed practical strategies to overcome these challenges, such as breaking tasks into smaller steps, setting realistic goals, and creating a distraction-free environment.

Building resilience is critical to overcoming challenges. Resilience involves bouncing back from setbacks, learning from failures, and moving forward. It's about viewing challenges as opportunities for growth and using them to strengthen your resolve and commitment to your goals.

Inspiring Future Success

As you progress, I encourage you to apply the principles discussed in this book to your life. Embrace hustle and discipline, commit to continuous learning, and stay resilient in facing challenges. By doing so, you can achieve your goals and create a fulfilling and successful life.

Success is not just about achieving your goals; it's about the journey and the person you become along the way. By embracing these principles, you can develop the skills, habits, and mindset needed to achieve lasting success and positively affect the world.

Vision for the Future

The potential for success is limitless. By embracing hustle, discipline, and continuous learning, you can achieve your dreams and create a future filled with opportunities and achievements. This book provides the tools and strategies to navigate this journey and reach your full potential.

Envision a future where you consistently achieve your goals, overcome challenges, and continuously improve. This future is within your reach, and by applying the principles discussed in this book, you can make it a reality. The journey to success begins with a single step, and this book provides the roadmap to guide you.

Final Thoughts and Call to Action

As we conclude this journey together, I want to leave you with a powerful thought: Success is not a destination but a journey. It's about the consistent effort, dedication, and resilience you bring daily. By embracing hustle and discipline and committing to continuous learning, you can achieve your goals and create a fulfilling and successful life.

I urge you to act today. Start by setting clear goals, creating a plan, and committing to the principles of hustle and discipline. Remember that success is a journey; every step you take brings you closer to your goals. Embrace the process, stay committed, and watch your efforts transform into remarkable achievements.

Long-Lasting Impact

The principles of hustle and learning can create a lasting impact on your life and the lives of those around you. By embracing these principles, you can leave a legacy of hard work, continuous improvement, and success. This legacy can inspire future generations and create a positive ripple effect in your community.

Remember that the journey to success is ongoing. It's about continually striving for excellence, staying adaptable, and embracing new challenges. By committing to this journey, you can achieve lasting success and meaningfully change the world.

Continuous Growth

The journey of hustle and success is never-ending. Continuous growth and improvement are essential for keeping long-term success. Stay curious, keep learning, and never stop striving for excellence. Doing so ensures that your success is sustainable and that you continue to achieve your goals.

Continuous growth involves seeking new opportunities, embracing change, and staying adaptable. It's about pushing your boundaries, taking calculated risks, and always seeking improvement. This mindset ensures that you are still competitive and practical in your efforts.

Embracing Change

Change is a constant in life; embracing it is crucial for long-term success. Stay open to new ideas, be willing to adapt, and always look for opportunities to innovate. By embracing change, you can stay ahead of the curve and continue to achieve your goals.

Innovation and adaptability are crucial to staying relevant and competitive. The world constantly evolves, and staying ahead requires embracing new technologies, ideas, and approaches. This adaptability ensures that you stay effective and successful in your efforts.

Leveraging Your Network

Building and using your network is essential for achieving long-term success. Surround yourself with like-minded individuals who share your goals and values. This network can provide support, advice, and opportunities, helping you achieve your goals and stay motivated.

Networking involves building relationships, seeking mentors, and collaborating with others. By using your network, you can gain valuable insights, support, and resources that enhance your efforts and help you achieve your goals.

Self-Care and Balance

Maintaining a healthy balance between work and self-care is crucial for long-term success. Take care of your physical and mental health, prioritize rest and relaxation, and ensure you have the energy and clarity to stay focused and productive.

Self-care involves setting boundaries, taking breaks, and engaging in activities that recharge your energy. By prioritizing self-care, you can prevent burnout, keep your motion, and ensure that hustle is your sustainable.

Setting Boundaries

Setting boundaries is an important part of disciplined hustle. Know when to say no to distractions and yes to opportunities that align with your goals. Boundaries ensure that your hustle stays focused and effective, allowing you to achieve your goals without becoming overwhelmed.

Boundaries involve prioritizing time and energy, managing distractions, and staying focused on your goals. By setting clear boundaries, you can ensure that your efforts still are aligned with your goals and that you stay productive and motivated.

Leveraging Technology

Technology can be a powerful ally in your hustle. Utilize productivity apps, time management tools, and other digital resources to streamline your efforts and stay organized. Technology can automate repetitive tasks, freeing more time for focused hustle and continuous improvement.

Leveraging technology involves staying updated with the latest tools and trends, seeking resources, and integrating technology into daily routines. This ensures that you stay effective, maximizing your productivity and results.

Celebrating Small Wins

Recognizing and celebrating small wins is crucial for supporting motivation and momentum. Acknowledge your progress, reward yourself for achievements, and stay motivated to continue your journey. Celebrating small wins reinforces your commitment and provides a sense of accomplishment.

Celebrating small wins involves setting milestones, tracking your progress, and taking time to reflect on. His reinforcement keeps you motivation and motivates you to stay focused and committed to your goals.

The Power of Routine

Routines create a rhythm that makes hustle automatic and discipline effortless. Establishing consistent routines ensures that your efforts are sustained and that you stay focused on your goals. Over time, these routines become second nature, seamlessly integrating hustle into your daily life.

Creating effective routines involves finding key activities, setting specific times for focused work, and minimizing distractions. By setting up and keeping routines, you can ensure that your efforts still are consistent and that your hustle is sustained over the long term.

Gratitude and Mindfulness

Practicing gratitude and mindfulness can transform your hustle experience. Focus on what you have and what you've achieved and appreciate the process as much as the outcome. Gratitude and mindfulness foster a positive mindset that makes the journey enjoyable and fulfilling.

Gratitude involves recognizing and appreciating your progress, expressing thankfulness for opportunities, and staying positive. Mindfulness consists of staying present, being aware of your thoughts and actions, and keeping focus. Together, these practices enhance your hustle and discipline.

Public Commitment

Publicly committing to your goals can strengthen your discipline and motivation. Sharing your goals with others creates a sense of accountability and increases your commitment to achieving them. This public commitment reinforces your resolve and makes your hustle more concrete.

Public commitment involves sharing your goals with friends, family, or colleagues, seeking accountability partners, and regularly updating others on your progress. This external accountability reinforces your internal discipline and enhances your efforts.

Flexibility in Approach

While discipline provides the structure, flexibility allows you to adapt to changing circumstances without losing momentum. Stay rigid in your goals but flexible in your methods. This balance ensures that you stay effective and adaptable in your efforts.

Flexibility involves being open to new ideas, adjusting your strategies as needed, and staying adaptable when facing challenges. By keeping flexibility, you can ensure that your efforts still are effective and stay on track toward achieving your goals.

Embracing Challenges

Challenges are opportunities for growth and learning. Embrace them with a positive mindset, view them as stepping stones to success, and use them to strengthen your resolve. Embracing challenges ensures that you stay resilient and motivated in your journey.

Embracing challenges involves staying positive, seeking solutions, and viewing setbacks as opportunities to learn and grow. This mindset ensures that you are still resilient and motivated, enabling you to overcome obstacles and achieve your goals.

Seeking Inspiration

Inspiration can provide the motivation and drive to stay committed to your goals. Seek sources of inspiration, whether through books, mentors, or experiences, and use them to fuel your hustle and discipline.

Seeking inspiration involves finding role models, reading success stories, and engaging in activities that inspire and motivate you. By staying inspired, you can stay motivated and focused on your journey to success.

Building Resilience

Resilience is the ability to bounce back from setbacks, learn from failures, and continue moving forward. Building resilience ensures you stay committed to your goals, even when faced with challenges and obstacles.

Building resilience involves developing a positive mindset, seeking support, and staying adaptable to challenges. This resilience ensures that you stay focused and motivated, enabling you to achieve long-term success.

The Journey of Self-Improvement

Self-improvement is an ongoing journey that continually looks to enhance your skills, habits, and mindset. Embrace this journey, stay committed to your growth, and strive for excellence.

The journey of self-improvement involves setting goals, seeking feedback, and regularly evaluating your progress. By staying committed to self-improvement, you can ensure that your efforts still are aligned with your goals and that you continue to grow and develop.

Leaving a Legacy

Your journey of hustle and success can leave a lasting legacy. Use your achievements to inspire and motivate others, create a positive impact in your community, and leave a legacy of hard work, continuous improvement, and success.

Leaving a legacy involves sharing your knowledge, mentoring others, and using your success to make a positive impact. This legacy can inspire future generations and create a positive ripple effect in your community.

Vision for the Future

Envision a future where you consistently achieve your goals, overcome challenges, and continuously improve. This future is within your reach, and by applying the principles discussed in this book, you can make it a reality. The journey to success begins with a single step, and this book provides the roadmap to guide you.

Envisioning your future involves setting long-term goals, creating a plan, and staying committed to your journey. By supporting a vision for your future, you can stay motivated and focused, ensuring you achieve your goals and create a fulfilling and successful life.

The Importance of Gratitude

Gratitude can transform your experience of hustle and success. Focus on what you have and what you've achieved and appreciate the process as much as the outcome. Gratitude fosters a positive mindset that makes the journey enjoyable and fulfilling.

Practicing gratitude involves recognizing and appreciating your progress, expressing thankfulness for opportunities, and staying positive. This positive mindset enhances your hustle and discipline, ensuring you stay motivated and focused.

The Power of Consistency

Consistency is key to achieving long-term success. Stay committed to your goals, support a high level of effort, and consistently strive for excellence. This consistency ensures that you make steady progress and achieve your goals over time.

Consistency involves setting routines, keeping discipline, and staying focused on your goals. By staying consistent, you can ensure that your efforts still are effective, that you achieve your goals, and that you create a fulfilling and successful life.

Final Call to Action

As we conclude this journey together, I urge you to act today. Start by setting clear goals, creating a plan, and committing to the principles of hustle and discipline. Remember that success is a journey; every step you take brings you closer to your goals. Embrace the process, stay committed, and watch your efforts transform into remarkable achievements.

Act today by setting clear goals, creating a plan, and committing to the principles of hustle and discipline. By doing so, you can achieve your goals and create a fulfilling and successful life. The journey to success begins with a single step, and this book provides the roadmap to guide you.

In conclusion, "Huge Only Comes Before Hustle in the Dictionary: How to Automatically Turn on Your Natural Training and Discipline to Succeed" is a comprehensive guide to achieving significant success through hard work, discipline, and continuous improvement. By applying the principles outlined in this book, you can harness your natural skills and habits to achieve your goals effortlessly and sustainably. The journey to success begins with hustle, and this book provides the tools and mindset needed to make that journey a reality.

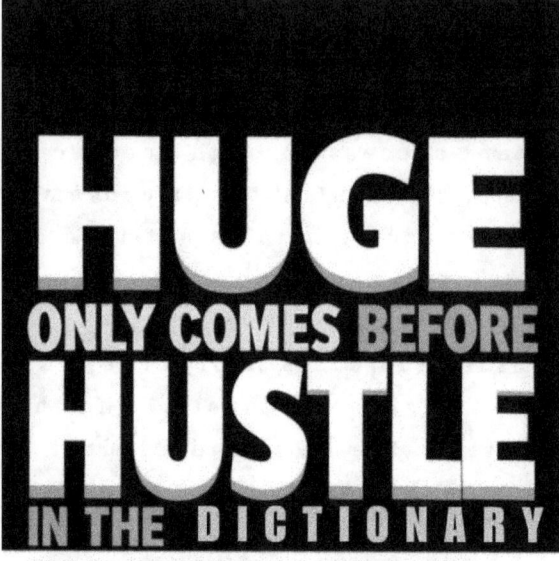

HUGE
ONLY COMES BEFORE
HUSTLE
IN THE DICTIONARY

HOW TO AUTOMATICALLY TURN ON YOUR NATURAL TRAINING & DISCIPLINE TO SUCCEED

Check Out A Book Bundle From
Brian's Other Famous Titles
"How To Get Past The Gatekeepers and
Get To Your Goal In Life:
A Personal Guide to Being Persistent"

Bibliography

1. **Covey, Stephen R.** *The 7 Habits of Highly Effective People: Powerful Lessons in Personal Change*. Simon & Schuster, 1989.

2. **Hill, Napoleon.** *Think and Grow Rich*. The Ralston Society, 1937.

3. **Kiyosaki, Robert T.** *Rich Dad Poor Dad: What the Rich Teach Their Kids About Money That the Poor and Middle Class Do Not!*. Plata Publishing, 1997.

4. **Tracy, Brian.** *Goals!: How to Get Everything You Want Faster Than You Ever Thought Possible*. Berrett-Koehler Publishers, 2003.

5. **Sinek, Simon.** *Start with Why: How Great Leaders Inspire Everyone to Take Action*. Portfolio, 2009.

6. **Dweck, Carol S.** *Mindset: The New Psychology of Success*. Ballantine Books, 2006.

7. **Vaynerchuk, Gary.** *Crush It!: Why NOW Is the Time to Cash In on Your Passion*. HarperStudio, 2009.

8. **Cardone, Grant.** *The 10X Rule: The Only Difference Between Success and Failure*. Wiley, 2011.

9. **Ferriss, Timothy.** *The 4-Hour Workweek: Escape 9-5, Live Anywhere, and Join the New Rich*. Crown Publishing Group, 2007.

10. **Thiel, Peter.** *Zero to One: Notes on Startups, or How to Build the Future*. Crown Business, 2014.

11. **Collins, Jim.** *Good to Great: Why Some Companies Make the Leap... and Others Don't*. HarperBusiness, 2001.

12. **Schultz, Howard, and Joanne Gordon.** *Onward: How Starbucks Fought for Its Life without Losing Its Soul*. Rodale Books, 2011.

13. **Maxwell, John C.** *The 21 Irrefutable Laws of Leadership: Follow Them and People Will Follow You*. Thomas Nelson, 1998.

14. **Sincero, Jen.** *You Are a Badass at Making Money: Master the Mindset of Wealth*. Viking, 2017.

15. **Dalio, Ray.** *Principles: Life and Work*. Simon & Schuster, 2017.

NOTES

www.ingramcontent.com/pod-product-compliance
Lightning Source LLC
Chambersburg PA
CBHW071928210526
45479CB00002B/593